Meandering Mind

Zoeb Kamdar

BookLeaf Publishing
India | USA | UK

Made with ❤ on the BookLeaf Publishing Platform
www.bookleafpub.in
www.bookleafpub.com

I dedicate this book to my mother, Batool Shamsuddin Kamdar, who gave me the freedom and the wings to experience life and fly as high as I dared to. And who stood there rock solid to hold me if I stumbled.

I miss you Mom.

Acknowledgement

I would like to acknowledge the four people who made it possible for me to share the meanderings of my mind which more often than not came out with a view of life, people, nature, events and situations as I saw and experienced them -

My son Dr. Husain Z Kamdar, who although far away from us still manages to care, love and push us to live our lives to the fullest.

Insiyah Z Kamdar, my wife who patiently tolerates my meandering, and often quirky mind, over the past 40 years together, and for appreciating everything that I wrote. No matter how much the words and thoughts meandered and managed to confuse her.

Dr. Munira A Khambaty who saw the therapeutic need for me to put down my thoughts, no matter how convoluted they were. Thank you for starting me on my journey with your gift of the leather-bound diary to pen my thoughts in. You wanted that diary as a gift. This book is your gift instead.

Ruby Mustan Calcuttawala who I call my guru and who ignited the dying embers of my creativity into roaring flames which encouraged me to dare attempt this book. Thank you Ruby for your faith in me and for gently pointing me in the right direction every time I needed your guidance. It kept the flame alive for creating this book. You wanted 15 poems from me. I hope these 40 bring a smile.

Preface

Meandering Mind is the outcome of my 69-year journey through life. *Meandering Mind* touches upon societal norms, Life, Nature, Love, the Elements, occasional humor and just about any day-to-day situation which caught my eye. The writing is in simple prose format and captures the flow of my mind often leaving the reader with questions and jiggling the mind to think in directions hitherto not thought about.

My Vision

You see

The sun rise

With all

Its heat

And discomfort.

I see

A new day

Filled with

Opportunities

To correct

My yesterdays

And move towards

My tomorrows.

You see

The rain

The wet

Ugly slush.

I see

The rain

Bringing

New life

In nature

Around us

Bringing with it

Hope for survival

For yet another year.

You see

The moon

And think

Of the calm

And the silence

It brings.

I see

The moon

And the opportunity

It brings

To rest

My mind

My body

For a new day

That promises

Opportunities

To correct

My yesterdays

And move

Towards

My tomorrows

With

The rising sun.

Meandering Mind-1

Is the beginning

The beginning

Or is

The end

A beginning?

End

Or

Beginning

Matters not

For both are

Beginnings.

The Hunt

Sun shining

Bright

Hot.

Gentle

Wind

Across

The face.

Keen eyes

Sweep the

Surroundings.

Movement

Down below

Wind whistling

Past

Feathers flattened

Talons out

Prey

Plucked

From the

Ground

In a flash

A dance

Of life

And death

The eagle

Master hunter

Has won

Once again.

Sounds of Silence

Vacant eyes

Staring

Out the

Window

Time

Stands still.

A sudden

Glimmer

Of fleeting

Memories

A wistful

Smile

As though

Wishing for

Days past

To return.

The head

Cocks

Hearing

Shrill sounds

Of children

Long flown

To make

Their Lives.

Weary bones

Carry

The aging

Body

From

Room to room.

Weary eyes

Look at

The walls

Adorned

With family

Long gone.

Creased Hands

Caress

Every piece

Of furniture

Remembering

Those

Who sat there once.

Oh this weary

Journey

Of old age

Through

The sounds

Of Silence.

Marriage & Acceptable Sin

An unknown

Being

Appointed by

An unknown being

Utters

A few words

Often unheard

Before

And

Oft not

Understood fully

By many

But still

Accepted

By All

And Lo

The sin

Becomes

Acceptable.

Meandering Mind-2

Sitting by

The seashore

Waves

Rolling in

Lapping

At feet

Gentle melody

Of receding

Waves

Carefree

Not a care

For the moment

I wonder

Where

Those days

Carefree

And

Innocent

Have gone.

Those days

Of

Senseless

Laughter;

Those days

Of

Unbridled

Mischief;

Those days

Of

Friendships

That

Endured

Insults

Fights

And

Instant

Patch-ups.

And

As the waves

Recede

Like those

Carefree days

I am saddened

That

The desperate

Desire

To conform

Has caused

The death

Of innocence.

Fire

A man

Ate

An apple

And

Paradise

Was lost

Did hellfire

Get created then?

One wonders.

Fire

The Universal

Creator

Of human

Ingenuity

In steel.

Fire

The gently

Creative

Creator

Of beauty

In precious

Metals.

Fire

Creator

Of

Beauty

In

Delicate

Glass.

Fire

The destroyer

Of humans

And of

Human creations.

Fire

Of hell

A tool

To strike

Fear

In the hearts

Of mankind.

The creator

And

The destroyer

Of life

As we

Know it

By fire

Of

The sun.

Stone

Stone

On

The wayside

An object

Ignored.

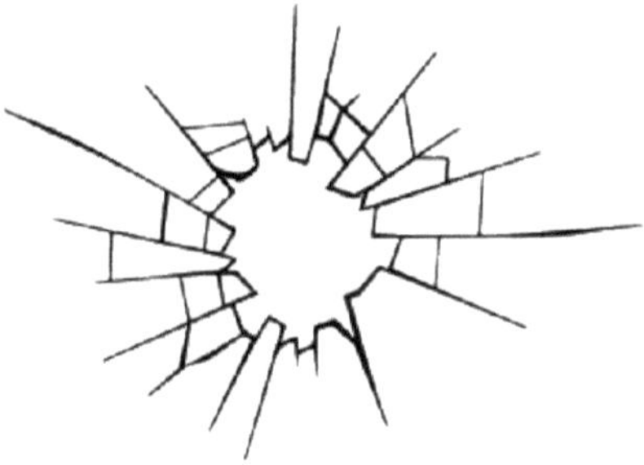

Stone

Flat

And shiny

Skipping

Joyously

On water.

Stone

In the

Way

To kick

In frustration.

Stone

In

The hands

Of

A sculptor

An object

Of beauty.

Stone

To cause

Destruction

In anger.

Stone

From

A beloved

Name

Written

A treasure

Forever.

Stone

Multifaceted

Beautiful

To the one

Who sees

Beauty

In a simple

Stone.

Paradise Lost-Covid

I was

A traveler

In

This world

Who

Sought only

His comfort

And the

Fulfillment

Of his

Needs

Destroying

The heaven

He was

Gifted.

And then

The heaven

Turned

On me

And said

ENOUGH

And the

Universe

Joined

Hands

To show

Me

The power

Of destruction

That I

Had invited

To turn

My heaven

Into hell.

Now I

Ask

The Universe—

What did

I do

Wrong?

What should

I now

Do?

And the

Universe

Answers

With its own

Questions—

What did you

Do right?

What should

You do now?

Look around you

And the answer

Is there

In

The purity

Of the air

The purity

Of the

Water

The purity

Of the

Silence

Which you

Had destroyed

Over a hundred

And more

Years

Which I

Have restored

In just

A few days

By keeping

You

Away

From my

Heaven.

(Written during the Covid lockdown when the air and water became purer without humans)

River

Lazily

Meandering

With

Gentle grace

Through

Valleys

And

Mountain

Base.

Reflecting

Skies

From

Dawn

To Dusk

Its journey

Long

And

Never done

Carrying

Life.

Finding

Its way

Through bends

And turns

A symbol

Of

Eternity

Of everlasting

Life

And

Its meandering.

Mumbai Local Train

I travel

By train

To reach

A destination

Known.

I travel

By train

In a crowd

Often pushed

Sometimes bruised

But

I reach

My destination

Through it all.

I travel

By train

Not knowing

The others'

Caste

Religion

Or beliefs

In life.

I tavel

By train

Making

New Friends

Of just

Fellow

Humans

On their

Journey.

I travel

By train

And I am

Reminded

Of life

And its journey

To a known

Destination

Death

Through

All the hardships

Making

New friends

With fellow

Humans

And Reaching

The final destination.

I travel

By train

And wonder

Why

The journey

Of life

Cannot be

Like

My journey

By train

Just fellow

Humans

Traveling to

Their

Final

Destination.

Meandering Mind - 3

Life

And

Death

Are both

Journeys

Unknown.

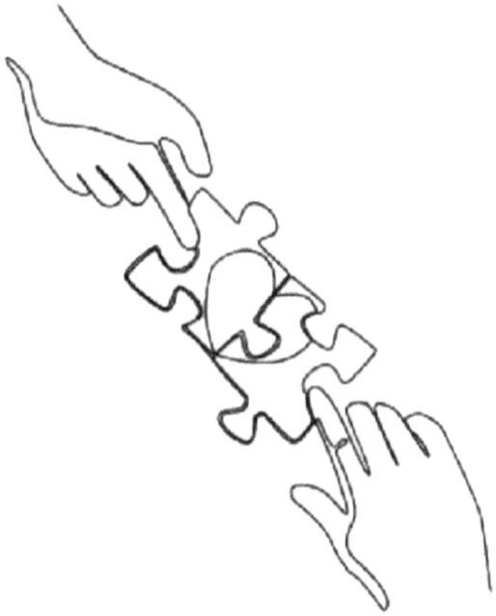

The Journey

Of both

Life

And

Death

Is to

Overcome

And

Succeed.

The beauty

Of both

Life

And

Death

Where

One

Is celebrated

The other

Is mourned.

The mind

Confounds

With the

Question:

Is Life the beginning

Of death

Or

Is death the beginning

Of Life?

Or

Are they

Eternally

Intertwined—

Just as

Day

Cannot be

Without

Night.

Heaven

The rising sun

Of early dawn

Pleasant warmth

Reminder of

New opportunities.

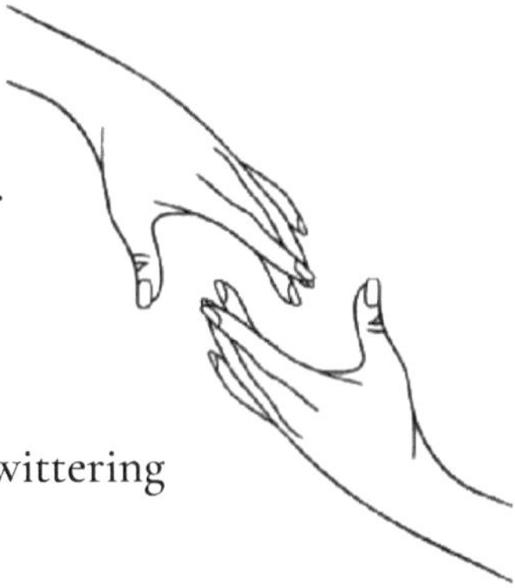

The chirping and twittering

Of winged creatures

Unseen but

The sounds of life

Awakening.

Gentle rustle

Of trees swaying

In the wind

A soothing lullaby.

Humming of

The early bee

Looking for nectar

In the bounty of

Colorful flowers.

Sounds of prayer

Aroma of coffee

Smells of a familiar

Morning meal

Mother's call

To the table.

Joyful and mischievous

Sounds of children

Rushing to school.

I think to myself

If there be a heaven

I am in it.

Lost Love

A love so true

Two hearts

Intertwined

Beating

As one.

Dreams and hopes

for a tomorrow

Together

In happiness and love.

Alas the love

So misunderstood

By the lovers

Tears apart

Two hearts

That were one.

Memories remain

Of hand in hand

Of lips on lips

Of endearments

Whispered

Of gifts of love

A love so true

Hopes so real

All memories of

A lost love.

The Stream

I sit

By

The stream

And

listen

To the

Gentle

Rippling

Of

The water

Like

Music

To the

Ears

And

I Wonder:

Has my

Being

Ever

Sounded

Like music

To Anyone?

I sit

By

The stream

And

listen

To the

Singing

Of

The songbirds

And

I Wonder:

Have I

Been

A song

In any

Heart?

I sit

By

The stream

And

listen

To the

Water

Flowing

And I

Pick

A pebble

Smooth

And shiny

And

I Wonder:

Have I

Flowed

In anyone's

Life

And

Smoothened

Their

Rough

Edges

And made

Them shine?

I sit

By

The stream

And

Look at

The

Teeming

Life

Along

Its path

And

I Wonder:

Have I

Created

A

Worthy

Life?

I sit

By

The stream

And wonder

If

Like

The stream

I too

Am destined

To be

Lost

In the ocean

Someday

With

Identity

Erased

And

The

Ocean

Enriched.

Independence

Country flag

Waving

Country flag

In the window

Country flag

In the car

Country flag

Pinned to chest

Independence

On display.

Independence

Gained

With so many

Sacrifices

Of sons

And daughters

Long since

Forgotten

Now.

The fight

For

Independence

Of thoughts

Of religion

Of words

Of men

Of women

Of children

Of values

Of rights

Forgotten

And

Reduced

To

Country flag

Waving

Country flag

In the window

Country flag

In the car

Country flag

Pinned to chest.

The sacrifices

All

In vain

In today's

Celebration

Of

Independence.

Friends

Friends

Like flowers

Of different

Hues

Some bright

Some unusual

With different

Fragrances

Some mild

Some strong

Some just

Like

A lingering

Memory.

Friends

Like flowers

Flourish

With

Love

And Care.

Friends

Are

Freedom—

To

Laugh

Tease

Fight

And yet

Travel together

In Life

As

Friends.

Ode to my Mother

Mom

Holding

My tiny

Fingers

Taught me

To walk.

Mom

With gentle

Chiding

Taught me

To talk

To thank

To say sorry.

Mom

Her lap

The best

Refuge

For my tired

Head

For my tears

At failure

In studies

And

Relationships.

Mom

Waiting up

Till

She sees

Me.

Mom

Praying for

My success

In all

I do

Praying

For my strength

To face

Failure

And

Rise again.

Mom

My mentor

My friend

My teacher

My best friend.

Mom

A whisper

A memory

An echo

In my

Heart

My world.

Success

Success

A crown

of

Roses

or

A crown

of

Thorns

Created by

Those

Upon whom

The wearer

May tread

With

Love

Or with

Anger.

Tread carefully

O success

Lest

The crown

Take your color

And turn

Roses

Into Thorns.

Mayfly

Gossamer wings

Bouncing sun rays

Into rainbow colors

Fluttering desperately

To leaves

To trees

Dancing on summer breeze

No time to pause

Every moment precious

Experiencing life

From dawn to dusk

Its short life

A lesson to all

Seize every moment

No matter how brief

To love

To live

To seize

The moment

Like

The mayfly.

The Handcart Puller

The sun

Blazing hot

Burning

On

His sweating back

He pulls

His groaning

Handcart.

The weight

Bends him

But

With rasping

Breath

He carries

On

His

Painful struggle

Dreaming of

A better

Life

His hands

Calloused

His feet

Weary

Yet

His dreams

Alive

His spirit

Unbroken

In his

World

Of toil.

The leaf

Gently floating

Through the soft

Wind

Wafting on

Waves

Unseen

The leaf

Falls

Far from

Its roots

To nourish

Another

Root.

The seed

A tiny

Unknown

Thing

Plucked by

Gravity

From

A tree

Or

A winged

Creature

As

Unsavoury

As

It

May seem

Becomes

In time

A giant

Bearing

Flowers

And fruits

All from

That tiny

Unknown thing:

The seed.

When I am gone

When

I am

Gone

Don't look

For me

In

Your memory;

Look

For me

In those

Who need

You

For I

Will dwell

In

Their

Grateful

Smiles.

When

I am

Gone

Don't look

For me

In

My pictures

You

Treasure;

Look

For me

In

The memories

You

Create

With

The young

And

The infirm.

When

I am

Gone

Don't look

For me

In

The gifts

I

Gave you;

Look

For me

In

Those

Who

Need

Those gifts

More

Than you.

When

I am

Gone

Don't look

For me

In my

Scent

Which lingers

In

My clothes;

Look

For me

In those

Who

Will treasure

Those

Clothes.

Look

For me

In those

Who need

All that

You

Can give

Of

Me

And

I

Will

Never

Be gone.

Rain

Sitting by

The window

Raindrops

Falling

Hazing

The vision

Pitter-patter

On gently

Swaying

Tree leaves

The gentle

Wind

Swinging

Blurred

Brightly hued

Flowers

Lulls the mind

With

Nature's

Lullaby.

The Orphan

Born

And

Abandoned

For reasons

Unknown

Growing up

With others

Unrelated

Not knowing

A name

A religion

A caste

A community

Just an

Abandoned

Human

Growing up

With no

Malice

Towards

Any religion

Any caste

Any community

Just a human

Living

In gratitude

With other

Humans

For

Whatever

Love

Is given

To

An abandoned

Human.

A Grain of rice

A tiny grain

From flooded fields

Pure and

White

Reaches

The steaming bowl

For

A simple meal

And a feast

For kings

A tiny grain

Of rice—

A life

For

So many.

Death

A journey

Feared

For

Its

Unknown

Unseen

Destination

A meeting

With

The MAKER

Only imagined

Creating

Fear

In the hearts

of

The living

Dead.

Sunbeam

Sunbeam

Piercing

Through

The Dawn

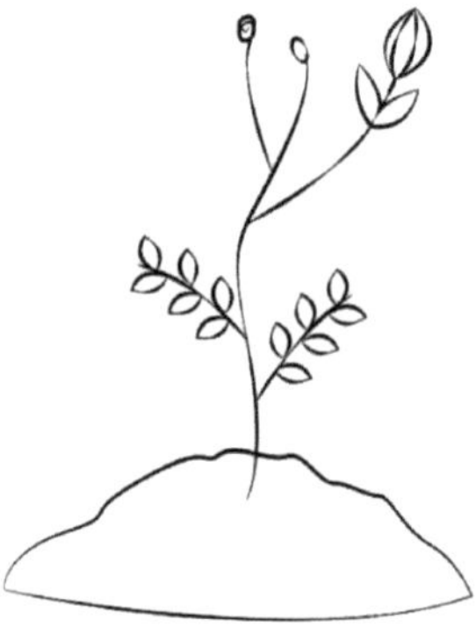

Touching

Dew

Drops

Glistening

Like

A million

Tiny

Diamonds

Till

The gentle breeze

Sways

The leaves

Dew drops

Dropping

Like

Tiny flashes

Of shining

Light.

Sunbeam

Lighting up

Waking up

The world

To

A new day

Of beauty

And

Of Colors

Brightened.

Child

A child's

Innocent

Laughter

Pure

Joyful

In every

Step

A new

Story

Unfolds.

No fear

No care

Dancing

In the

Rain

Singing

With

Joy.

Tiny hands

Transfer

Love

To all

They Touch.

A child

Brings

Hope

And

Memories

Of

Innocence

We have

Lost.

Tongue

Soft

Piece

Of

Flesh

Delicate

Tiny

Buds

Taste

Flavors

Oft times

Sweet

Sometimes

Sour

And

Bitter too

Occasionally

Like an

Arrow

In fleeting

Flight

Freed

From the

Taut Bowstring

Piercing

Hearts

Breaking

Them

Into

Pieces

That

Never

Join

Again.

Waiting at the Airport

Sitting in

A sea

Of glass

Muted

Announcements

The world

Going by

I sit

Listening

To the

Hum of

People

Engines

Strangers

Meeting briefly

Exchanging

Stories

Which will

Fade

With their

Parting.

Sitting in

A sea

Of glass

Muted

Announcements

Watching people

Some happy

Some anxious

Some first-timers

Nervous

I wait

For the skies

To call

Me

And let

The world

Fade away

As I

Find

My space

In

The skies.

Prayers

I

Close

My eyes

Lift

My hands

In silent

Prayer

Wondering

If

Someone

Is hearing

The voice

Of

My heart.

I

Close

My eyes

Lift

My hands

In silent

Prayer

Wondering

Why

I get

No answer.

I

Close

My eyes

Lift

My hands

In silent

Prayer

My mind

Wandering

Thinking

Of

My worldly

Woes

Desires

And

Wants.

I

Close

My eyes

Lift

My hands

In silent

Prayer

And then

I know

HE

Does not

Give

What I

Ask for

HE

Gives me

The strength

And direction

To

Fulfill

All

I

Need.

I

Close

My eyes

Lift

My hands

In silent

Prayer

And know

HE

Is with

Me.

My Child

As the

Sun sets

On

The horizon

Of

My life

I sit

And

Ponder.

My

Youth

I gave

To

Your

Care

Your

Happiness

Your

Desires

Your

Dreams

Your

Every

Want

No

Questions

Ever.

Now

You have

Grown

And

I sit

Pondering

Where

I erred

When you

Question

My every

Act

My every

Query

My every

Thought.

I am

Angry

Frustrated

At

Your questions

And

I ponder—

Is this

The

Generation gap

People

Talk of?

Or

Is this

Just

Your way

Of

Learning

From

My answers

And

Growing

To be

Better

Than me

Because then

I am

Glad

For all

The

Questions

From

The one

Who will

Always

Be

My child.

Through the eyes of a dog

How strange

You Humans

Having

Four limbs

But using

Two to

Walk

Leaving the

Other two

Hanging

Uselessly

Occasionally

Shaking one

With

A

Friend

Or

Banging them

Together

To make

Frightening Sounds.

How strange

You Humans

Stretching

Your lips

In happiness

Instead of

Anger

Like I do.

How Strange

You Humans

Using your

Two useless

Limbs

To

Fight

Instead

Of

Your teeth

Like me.

How strange

You Humans

Using your

Two useless

Limbs

Instead

Of

Your mouth

To

Carry weight.

How strange

You humans

To hold

Your

Emotions

Your

Wants

Your

Urgent needs

For want

Of

A private place.

How strange

You humans

Who

Think

I am

Strange

And cute.

(Written in one of those quirky mischievous moments)

Fly like a bird

Flying

Like a

Bird

Soaring

High above

With

The clouds

Looking

Down

At

The world

Below

Passing by

In a

Flash

Feeling the

Wind

And the

Freedom

From

Life's

Burdens

Oh how I wish

I could

Fly

Like

A bird.

Traffic

Sitting

In

Traffic

Waiting

For

The light

To Turn

Green

But

Oh, so quickly

It turns

From

Green to red

I could

Have had

A meal

Right then.

The light

Turns green

The car

In front

Stalls

The car

Behind

Honks

The light

Turns red.

I want

To tell

The guy

Behind,

"Buddy

We are

All trapped;

Honking

Won't do

The trick."

The GPS

Lies

It says

Fifteen minutes

Just as it did

When I left

From home.

I can sit

There cursing

Wishing

I had

Wings

Instead

I put on

Music

Sighing

At

This losing

Battle

With traffic

Hoping

To reach

My destination

Soon

Someday.

My Mobile

My mobile

Has

A funny

Bone

I say

"Call my wife"

It says

"Get a life".

My mobile

Seems to have

A mind

Of its own

And changes

"Love"

To

"Shove"

Its autocorrect

Is so

Often

Incorrect.

My mobile

Is always

There

Even when

I don't

Want it

And when

I do

Its

Battery dies.

My mobile

And me

We stick

Together

Right or Wrong

It's sometimes

Slow

And dumb

But

Without

My mobile

There's no fun.

My Diet

My day

Started

With a plan

So bold:

I'll eat

Only greens

And

Salads.

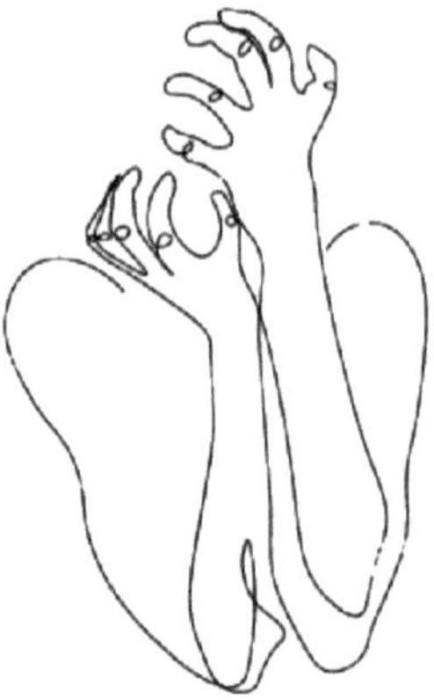

I started

With

A smoothie

So fresh

And thick

And of course

Green too

But come

Mid-morning

The hunger

Struck

It whispered

"Burger"

I fought

The whisper

But

By noon

The burger

Was calling.

One small

Bite

And then

One more

And soon

The floor

Was covered

With the crumbs

Of my regret.

By dinner

I swore

Tomorrow

For sure

But

The

Chocolate mousse

Did me in.

I say

To myself

Tomorrow's

Another

Chance

To chase

The dream

Of being

Slim and lean

So tonight

I'll enjoy

Till

I decide

To dare

Dream of greens

Again.

Sleep

As dusk

Sets in

And

Stars blink

The moon

Keeps watch

With

Its gentle

Glow

The mind

Is at

Ease

Time

Stands

Still

Worries

Of the world

Drift away

You are

Free

To roam

The world

Of dreams

And embrace

The gift

Of

Blessed sleep.

9 789363 300934

Printed by Libri Plureos GmbH in Hamburg, Germany